KIDS in JAIL

KIDS in JAIL

Andy Hjelmeland

Photographs by Dennis Wolf

Lerner Publications Company / Minneapolis

Library of Congress Cataloging-in-Publication Data

Hjelmeland, Andy.
    Kids in jail / Andy Hjelmeland ; photographs by Dennis Wolf.
        p.   cm.
    Includes bibliographical references
    Summary: Text and photographs describe the inner workings of the
juvenile justice system, focusing on a young offender's arrest, jailing, court
appearance, and time spent at the Minnesota Correctional Facility at
Red Wing.
    ISBN 0-8225-2552-6
    1. Juvenile delinquents—Minnesota—Interviews—Juvenile literature.
2. Minnesota Correctional Facility—Red Wing—Pictorial works—Juvenile
literature. 3. Juvenile justice, Administration of—Minnesota—Juvenile
literature. [1. Juvenile delinquents. 2. Minnesota Correctional Facility—
Red Wing. 3. Jails. 4. Justice, Administration of.] I. Wolf, Dennis, ill.
II. Title.
HV9105.M65H54   1992
364.3'6'09776—dc20   91-19454
                                                                CIP
                                                                AC

Manufactured in the United States of America

1 2 3 4 5 6 7 8 9 10 01 00 99 98 97 96 95 94 93 92

Acknowledgments

I want to thank my friend and colleague, Dennis Wolf, for his photographic skills and amiable companionship. As we traveled from one correctional facility to another, Dennis was steadily clicking away with his camera. His keen instinct for capturing these somber slices of institutional life make words unnecessary. His photos tell the story by themselves.

The many kids with whom I rubbed elbows must remain nameless. To John, I owe a debt of gratitude for his willingness to share some of the pain.

I also wish to thank the officials of Hennepin and Meeker Counties and the state of Minnesota for their cooperation. Gratitude, as well, to our young models Meghan Guernsey and Bunky Dahlquist, and to Bunky's parents, Mark and Suzie Dahlquist, for their generous contributions of time and effort. In no particular order, the following individuals also offered invaluable assistance: Art Cavara, Joe Heinze, Robert Mowatt, Rich Wheaton, Tom Lavelle, Norbert Gernes, Jerry Vitoff, Gerald O'Rourke, Judge John Weyrens, and deputy Bruce Dicke.

Two veterans of the juvenile justice system, whose expertise proved crucial, merit special mention: Joe Spano of the Hennepin County Probation Department, who opened doors and rendered assistance at the very beginning of this project (when I most needed it); and Minnesota Appellate Judge Gary L. Crippen, who researched and provided critical insights into the hodgepodge legalisms of the juvenile justice system.

To all of you, as well as the many unidentifiable folks not mentioned here, Dennis and I express our heartfelt appreciation for your kindly cooperation.

Author's Note

As far back as I can remember, I was always in trouble. In school, with the police, with my parents. At the age of four, I was caught stealing a candy bar—the first dark cloud in what would become a very stormy future. During my teens and early adulthood, I spent over 10 years in a variety of jails: reform schools, work farms, city and county lockups, and prisons. From shoplifting and vandalism, I moved on to burglary and armed robbery.

My behavior puzzled me as much as it did those around me. I wasn't a "bad" kid. I loved my parents. I wasn't vicious or hurtful. I knew I was different, but I never did sort out the reasons for my rebellious nature. Although it's been 26 years since the last jail door clanged shut behind me, the time I spent behind bars left an unforgettable impression.

What I remember most are the young lives that got caught up, as mine did, in the treadmill of the correctional system. Even now I hear from men I first met in reform schools in the 1950s who are still doing time in prison.

I was lucky. I escaped the revolving door of the correctional system. Currently more than half a million convicts are in United States prisons, and many of these people are in prison for the second, third, fourth, or fifth time. While researching this book, I realized that some of the young people I spoke with would end up following the same path.

The intention of this book is not to scold or to preach. It is simply to furnish a glimpse into the inner workings of the juvenile justice system.

A young offender named John is the guiding voice of this book. He is an inmate at the Minnesota Correctional Facility at Red Wing. During interviews, he talked about his family, being arrested, going to jail, appearing in court, and spending time in reform school. I thank him for his cooperation.

Out of respect for the privacy of the young people in these institutions, models were used in the photographs in which faces are shown.

My whole family is kind of screwy," John says with a self-conscious smile. "I've had four stepfathers. One of them was *supposed* to be my real father, according to my mother. Then one day I asked her, 'How can this guy be my father? He don't look like me, he don't act like me, and he hates my guts.' So she finally admitted my real father was in a penitentiary in Washington."

John eventually contacted his biological father. "He's out now but doesn't seem interested in seeing me. I wrote to him and even talked to him on the telephone. I guess he's got his own life to live. I won't bother him no more..."

John is a handsome 17-year-old who is serving time in the Minnesota Correctional Facility at Red Wing. He's friendly and soft-spoken. He doesn't look or act like a juvenile delinquent. But then, neither do most of the other 100 boys confined at Red Wing. When they speak, however, the differences between these boys and "straight" kids become obvious.

A husky 15-year-old boasts, "I been robbing and fighting since I was little. The first time I got arrested I was 10."

Another boy speaks casually of his exploits: "I was running with gangs when I was 14. We stole cars and robbed and used marijuana, cocaine, LSD, mushrooms. We did a lot of drinking, too."

"I got this real bad temper," a 16-year-old says. He seems puzzled by this trait. "When I get mad I just, like...lose it. I stabbed a couple people. It's good I didn't have a gun."

Many kids who are in trouble with the law lack a stable family life. The young men at Red Wing talk about being shuttled among grandparents, aunts, uncles, and foster homes while they were growing up. Many are from single-parent homes. The boys' conversation about the adults in their lives is sprinkled with tales of drug use, heavy drinking, divorce, and violence.

As he peers out the window at a group of fellow inmates returning from a work detail, John muses on his childhood.

"When my mother gets drunk, she fights with everybody around her. She used to yell at me for getting into trouble, and she acted worse than me. Even when I was small she used to tell me I'd end up in Red Wing. If she wasn't my mother, I wouldn't care if I ever saw her again."

Like many correctional facilities, the one at Red Wing looks more like a college campus than a jail.

Most people have never seen the inside of a jail. Our ideas about jails come mainly from movies and television. The word "jail" may bring to mind dark, dungeon-like cells, high stone walls topped with gun towers, and lots of tough-looking characters swaggering around. Places like this do exist. But many jails have no bars or high walls. Some resemble summer camps or army barracks.

Institutions for criminals—juveniles as well as adults—are called *correctional facilities*. This is simply a fancy name for jail. A correctional facility is a building that holds people who are either suspected of or have been convicted of committing a crime. People who are convicted (found guilty) may be sent to other kinds of jails, such as prisons, penitentiaries, reformatories, or chain gangs. Slang terms have often been used to describe these places, such as "the slammer," "the joint," "the pokey," or "the cooler."

Nearly 100,000 people under the age of 18 are confined in juvenile institutions in the United States. In most states, anyone under the age of 18 is considered a juvenile. Unless juveniles commit a very serious crime, such as murder, they are not confined in the same buildings as adults.

Murder, robbery, assault (a violent attack), and destruction of property are criminal acts, no matter who commits them, adults or young people. Serious crimes such as these are called *felonies*.

"Status offenses," however, are not crimes unless a juvenile commits them. Curfew violations, frequent truancy (missing school), underage drinking, and running away from home are status offenses. Occasionally, parents who cannot control their children turn them over to the police as "incorrigible," another status offense.

Males commit far more crimes than females. More than 85 percent of all juveniles arrested for committing felonies are males. Males are also responsible for the great majority of violent crimes (assault and murder). In long-term juvenile institutions, 93 percent of the inmates are boys.

Girls do account for about half of all arrests for status offenses. At present, nearly 20,000 female juveniles are in custody in the United States.

Because girls tend to commit less serious crimes, they are more often sent to shelters and group homes rather than long-term institutions. But some girls also commit serious crimes and get sent to the same kinds of correctional facilities as boys. Boys and girls may be held in the same facility, but with separate living quarters.

Most juveniles are released into the custody of their parents soon after their arrest. If they have been in trouble before, they might be kept in a juvenile detention center until they go to court. Some will eventually be sent to long-term correctional facilities, such as the institution in Red Wing where John is serving his time.

Homemade tattoos form a haphazard pattern along John's muscular forearm. The letters "L-O-V-E" are imprinted on each finger of one hand between the knuckles and joints. John studies the tattoo for a moment, his long blond hair falling loosely across his face.

"I done that in here." He shrugs. "Someday I'll probably regret it. Like a lot of things I done."

More than a million juveniles under the age of 18 are arrested each year in the United States. Theft is the most common crime.

"When I was little, I did a lot of shoplifting," John says. "I also stole from the tavern my mother owned. People would leave money laying around and I'd grab it."

Most youths who end up in institutions begin stealing at an early age—often as young as five or six. By the time they appear in juvenile court, they usually have been involved in several incidents of theft. The crimes tend to become more serious with age.

Most delinquents also have problems in school. John says he was kicked out of school often, starting in fourth grade. "Mostly for fighting and talking back to teachers. I always got in a lot of fights."

John was 15 when he was arrested for a series of felonies. "We stole cars and robbed a bunch of houses. Me and my friends had a garage full of stuff we stole. One night we went up to this house and took two snowmobiles. We got in a chase with the cops. I crashed into a barbed wire fence and got cut up pretty good. I hid outside in the snow for about three hours before they caught me."

When a juvenile like John is arrested, he is first taken to the local police station. His parents are notified and he might be released to them until a court date is scheduled. Or he may be taken to a detention center, or juvenile center, often called "JC."

Except for the sign above the entrance—"Hennepin County Juvenile Center"—it's hard to tell that this downtown building is a jail. From the outside, it looks like any other Minneapolis office building. There are no steel bars or iron grates over the windows.

The journey through the juvenile justice system begins with the arrest. A police officer handcuffs the suspect and takes him to the police station, where he is booked.

But the front entrance leading into the waiting room is the only door without a heavy-duty lock. Along one wall, a uniformed officer sits behind a large, plate-glass enclosure. This is the control room, where the sights and sounds of the entire building are monitored. Cameras and an intercom system provide instant communication with every part of the building. To get from one area to another, visitors and workers must pass through a maze of locked doors. The juvenile detention center is a maximum-security facility, as escape-proof as most adult jails.

At the juvenile center, the suspect is searched for weapons and drugs. All his belongings and street clothes will be stored until the court decides his case. In the center, the offender is required to wear "scrubs"—loose-fitting blue smocks.

The next stop for the suspect is the juvenile detention center. Security at "JC" is extremely tight.

"JC is mostly sitting around," John says. "There's the usual stuff—checkers, cards, TV. And you get to go outside in this fenced-in playground a couple times a day. There's school, too. Mostly, though, it's just sitting around between taking tests and talking to social workers."

In the U.S., adult laws and court proceedings are governed by the Constitution. Certain rights, such as trial by jury, are guaranteed under the Bill of Rights.

Young people, however, do not have the same rights. The juvenile justice system is not required to follow the laws that are protected by the Constitution. As a result, juvenile court procedures vary from state to state, county to county, and city to city.

A legal concept called *parens patriae*—Latin words that mean "King as parent"—forms the basis of modern juvenile law. The law has been interpreted to mean that when a child's natural parents cannot control the child, the government becomes the legal parent. The courts try to shield children from some of the legal machinery of the adult criminal system, and certain protections are granted to juvenile offenders. For example, their names cannot be revealed; their court hearings are not open to the public; and their court records are sealed, or private.

A juvenile hearing is a trial without a jury—an informal discussion about the facts of the case. Witnesses, the officer who made the arrest, and the accused person might testify at the hearing. Then the judge delivers a verdict of guilty or innocent.

If the young person is found guilty, his background is investigated. The seriousness of the crime is considered as well as the number of previous arrests. Parents are interviewed to find out about the person's home life. Tests are given to evaluate personality and intelligence. Before the judge can decide what should be done, many questions must be answered: Does the person have a drug or alcohol problem? A tendency toward violence? Mental instability? Based on this background information, the judge must decide what treatment is best for the offender as well as for society.

After the judge delivers a verdict of "guilty," he or she must decide what kind of a sentence the juvenile will serve.

Kids who break the law may end up in any of several kinds of institutions, from reform schools to jails.

When John first appeared in court for sentencing three years ago, the judge sent him to the Austin Boys Ranch for 9 to 12 months. John felt this was too harsh. He had hoped to be placed on probation. Being on probation is like having an extra parent—only a much stricter one.

"It was my first time in court," John recalls. "All the other times [I was arrested] I got released to my mother. When they sent me to Austin, I thought, 'You got to be kidding!'" He pauses. "I guess it was because of the number of crimes I done and all the fights I got into at JC. They figured I was a bad risk."

Judges have a baffling number of choices when they sentence juveniles. Besides state and county facilities, there are group homes, treatment centers, foster homes, camps, ranches, and psychiatric hospitals. In Minnesota, for example, more than 200 possible treatments are available for juvenile offenders.

An offender who is placed on probation must meet with a probation officer regularly.

In most cases, first offenders are placed on probation. On probation, young people must follow certain rules. If they break those rules, they risk being sent to an institution. Regular visits to the probation officer are required. A probation officer is someone the court assigns to supervise the young person. The officer closely watches the person's school attendance, behavior, and grades. He or she must get permission from the probation officer for many privileges, such as getting a driver's license, staying out later than the curfew, accepting or quitting a job, and traveling outside the state.

The alternative to probation is "residential treatment." Again, the judge decides which type of facility best suits the individual.

Almost 2,500 years ago, the Greek philosopher Socrates complained that the younger generation was not as well behaved as when he was a young man. Adults have always worried about young people's behavior. In 1921 a magazine writer commented, "No age has had such a problem of reckless and rebellious youth."

Throughout history, alarms have been sounded about juvenile crime. "They steal from their parents, swipe junk, pawn their clothes, do any desperate thing to get dope." This was written in a newspaper article 70 years ago. The drug problem is certainly more serious than ever before—but it's not new. Gangs are not a recent development, either. Without question, today's statistics are grim. Gang-related violence is at an all-time high. But 100 years ago, New York City had more and bigger gangs.

In the past, juvenile and adult criminals were treated in the same way. Two hundred years ago in England, for example, young people were put in jails with dangerous adult criminals. Sometimes children were even hanged.

Until recently, physical punishment was commonly used to discipline young people. In most correctional facilities today, the goal is rehabilitation—through education, job training, self-help programs, and therapy.

Juvenile jails used to be called "reform schools." But over the years, fancier names were invented. Now we have camps, ranches, refuges, and protectories.

Juvenile facilities are categorized as either "open environments" or "institutional environments." They differ in the amount of freedom allowed within the facility and the amount of contact permitted with the outside community. Open environments, such as camps, ranches, and group homes, allow greater freedom. Institutional environments are usually run by state or local governments. These places are for kids who need strict supervision.

John was sentenced to the Austin Boys Ranch, an open environment facility. But he ran away from Austin after a short stay.

"I took off from Austin," John explains, "because I didn't want to spend Christmas there and I wanted to see my girlfriend."

Runaways from open environment institutions almost always end up in a long-term reform school. The tighter restrictions at a reform school make it more difficult to "rabbit," or escape. When John was caught, he was sent to the Minnesota Correctional Facility at Red Wing.

Strict rules are enforced at a juvenile detention center.

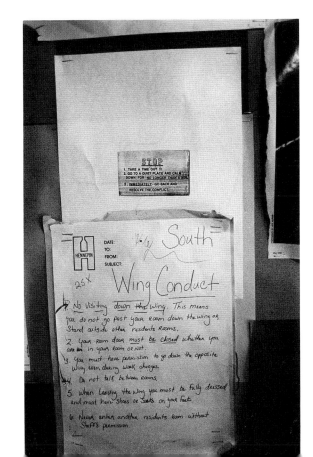

Most of the guys here," John says about Red Wing, "have been around the block a couple times." In other words, they have been in trouble with the law before and are familiar with juvenile jails.

The Red Wing Correctional Facility is a sprawling 200-acre complex located in a hilly area overlooking the Mississippi River valley. Built over 100 years ago, the facility is much like the long-term reform schools that exist in every state. Red Wing houses older, repeat offenders (those who have been in some kind of institution before), as well as runaways from open institutions (like John). The superintendent of Red Wing, Gerald O'Rourke, says, "Many of them have worn out their welcome at other placements."

Even though Red Wing is one of the most secure juvenile jails in the state, at first glance it looks like a college campus. There are no bars or fences. Staff members keep a close check on each inmate's comings and goings. (Inmates are referred to as "residents" by the staff.) No one is allowed to roam around unattended at Red Wing.

Seven cottages house the 100 juveniles and 80 adults confined at Red Wing. The adults are men who are nearing the end of prison terms. They have been sent to Red Wing to finish their sentences under less restrictive conditions. For these men, Red Wing functions as a "halfway house"—halfway between prison and free society. The men's activities are kept separate from those of the juveniles.

Inside a cottage at a reform school

Twenty-five inmates live in each cottage at Red Wing. Boys are assigned to cottages according to their degree of "sophistication." The older, more streetwise boys are separated from the younger, less savvy ones. Most of the boys are from large cities and are repeat offenders who have already spent time in county homes.

John sums up the boys at Red Wing. "Compared to other places, there's more bad dudes here—like gang members and guys who done heavier crimes."

Educational opportunities exist at Red Wing for those who choose to take advantage of them. The young men take high school courses such as algebra and English. Training is also offered in auto mechanics, welding, and art.

Although there aren't any girls at Red Wing, most state correctional facilities house both boys and girls.

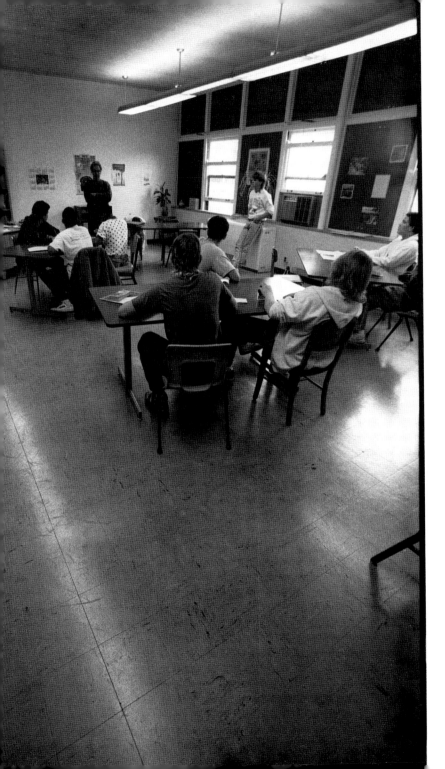

"I earned a GED [high school diploma] this time around," John says proudly. "I feel pretty good about that, like I finally accomplished something worthwhile. I even thought about college someday."

John and the other residents must keep to a tight schedule at Red Wing: they are up at six in the morning for breakfast—which they cook themselves—and a thorough cleaning of the cottage. Then they are off to school. Full-time school is required for all the boys, regardless of their age.

After school and on weekends, many of the boys participate in athletics. Basketball, volleyball, softball, and football are popular. Young men from different cottages compete against each other in intramural sports contests. Other boys prefer to spend their spare time watching television or reading. Off-grounds activities are highly prized privileges. Occasionally, an entire cottage is taken into town to attend a movie or use the swimming pool at the local school.

Probably the most important program at Red Wing is the "group meeting." Its purpose is to help the boys understand themselves better and sort out their feelings and conflicts. Superintendent O'Rourke emphasizes the importance of these meetings: "That's what this whole place is about."

After the evening meal, each cottage holds its own group meeting, conducted by a staff member. The boys evaluate each other's progress in setting and achieving personal goals.

"You get to unload a lot of stuff that bothers you," John says. "Like if another kid bugs you for some reason, you can bring it up and the whole group talks about it... But there's a lot of phoniness, too. You know, guys who act one way in front of the group and act totally different away from it."

If he were in charge, what changes would he make?

"I'd hire people who been in trouble and, you know, straightened out. People who been through this in their own life. Like in AA where everybody's an ex-drunk. Kids would listen more to somebody like that."

An inmate's behavior and attitude determine how long he will be confined. The average stay at Red Wing is about six months. Before a boy is released, living accommodations on the outside must be arranged. Juveniles are not allowed to live on their own; they must live with an adult—a parent, guardian, or relative.

"When I get out this time," John says, "I'll probably live with my grandma. I don't want to go back with my mother and the guy she's with now. It'd just be the same old thing. Arguing and fighting."

For many Red Wing residents, this is their last stop before reaching the age of 18, when the law will consider them adults. In Minnesota, the next rung up the correctional ladder is the state reformatory at St. Cloud—a gray fortress of granite walls, guard towers, and individual cells—or the state prison at Stillwater. Many of the convicts at St. Cloud and Stillwater spent portions of their adolescence in "kid joints," as these men refer to juvenile facilities.

The state reformatory in
St. Cloud, Minnesota, is a
maximum-security prison
for adults. On Sundays,
families—including babies
—are allowed to visit.

The hopes and dreams of the boys at Red Wing probably aren't much different from those of teenagers anywhere. Some dream big (of becoming famous actors or professional athletes), while most would settle for holding a steady job and raising a family. John loves music—he plays guitar and writes music—and fantasizes about becoming a professional musician someday.

"I know it's a long shot, but I think everybody needs some, like, goal to shoot at. Even if you don't make it, well, at least you tried. The first thing I got to do, though, is stay out of jail."

Bibliography

The source for statistics cited about juvenile crime is the *Sourcebook of Criminal Justice Statistics—1989*, published by the United States Department of Justice. Another source of information was the U.S. Justice bulletin "Children in Custody."

Other books about jail include:

Kosof, Anna. *Prison Life in America.* New York: Franklin Watts, 1984.

Richard, Graham. *Prisons and Punishment.* New York: Bookwright Press, 1987.

Robins, David. *Just Punishment.* New York: Gloucester Press, 1990.

Andy Hjelmeland knows firsthand what it's like to spend time behind bars. As a young man, he spent many years in correctional institutions. Hjelmeland first began to write in prison and now earns a living as a writer. He has published articles in *Newsweek*, *Sports Illustrated*, the *Minneapolis Star Tribune*, *The Nation*, and *Mother Earth News*. He is also the author of the children's book *Drinking and Driving*. Hjelmeland lives in Minneapolis.

Dennis Wolf is a freelance photographer and an art director at Webb Publications in Minneapolis. He has also worked as a cartoonist and illustrator. Besides photography, Wolf enjoys book collecting and audio and video production.